SHIFT TO LIGHT

90 DAYS TO GRATEFUL

RACHEL DESROCHERS

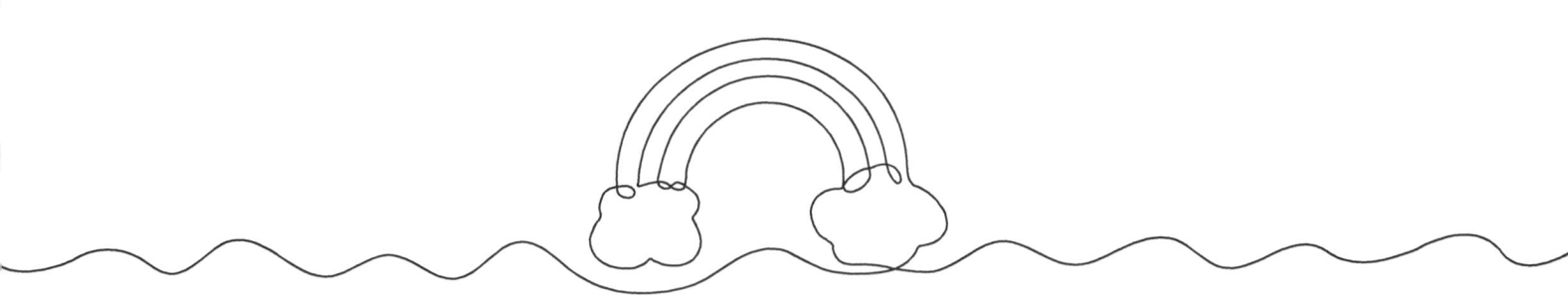

Shift to Light: 90 Days to Grateful
Copyright © 2024 by Rachel DesRochers

Published by VITALITY buzz, bliss + books LLC
vitalitybuzz.org

Proceeds from sales of this book benefit the mission of VITALITY Cincinnati Inc: transforming lives through holistic self-care from neighborhood to neighborhood, person to person, and breath by breath since 2010. It's the power of the circle!

The ideas expressed herein are those of the author and do not necessarily represent the opinions of the staff or Board of Trustees of VITALITY Cincinnati or VITALITY buzz, bliss + books LLC. Any errors, of course, are solely the author's.

Every effort has been made to give credit to other people's original ideas within the text. If you feel something should be credited to someone and is not, please get in touch through our website and every effort will be made to correct this text for future printings. Thank you!

We invite you to honor your mind, your body, your whole self. Do only what you know to be right for you. While the invitations offered here in this book, on our websites and social media, and in our classes are geared to be gentle and easily modified by the participant to fit the participants' needs, please consult your medical doctor or health professional before undertaking any practices.

ISBN: 978-1-954688-23-0
Library of Congress Control Number: applied for

This journal is dedicated to my dad, Gerry Grubbs.

Thank you, for being a great dad
& reminding me of this practice at every turn.

Thank you for always being here.
I love you so much.

**In gratitude to our VATRONS
who seek with us all a new way forward &
who have helped bring forward this new volume
by pre-ordering their copy — we thank you!**

Marla Barone, Gretchen Bayer, Stephanie Beck Borden, Amy Benetti,
Lauren Boehm, Lauren Boehmker, Holly Brians Ragusa, Rita Brooks,
Pam Cho, Sara Clifton, Kerry Conley, Alison Crowdus, Kimberly Darpel,
Karen Deime, Julie Doepke, Jennifer Dreyer, Lisa Dugan-Manor,
Amie Duncan, Denise Fenik, Lorrie Hayes, Tara Heilman, Mary Huss,
Jesse Kelly, April Kline, Claire Krawsczyn, Stephanie Kruthaupt,
Brianna Ledsome, Cathy Lindemann, Tara Litmer, Teah Longland,
Catherine Manabat, Stacey McIntyre, Meghan Metzger, Kelley Moore,
Nickol Mora, Krista Powers, Brian Shircliff, Rakhi Srivastava, Aly Stacy,
Theresa Wilmot, Lauren Worley, Cynthia Wright Sellers, Kate Zink

I remember during an interview once someone asked me what my favorite sound was.

Never had I been asked that question and never have I been asked that question again.

When I finally had an answer it was this:

My favorite sound is the Inhale that someone has to take when asked the question - what are you grateful for today?

If you are still and listen, you can hear it, you can feel it. The moment that stillness enters in and you get present. See, to tell me what you are grateful for you can't push through that, you can't just shout out a response. You have to take a breath in, you have to receive the question, you have to get back in your body.

This book, these prompts, are a daily tool to get you back into your body. There are prompts meant for every day, but some of those are just moments of stillness, the "take notice" prompts as I am calling them. Nothing to do but learn to be.

This practice.
This journal.
This work.

It is my life, and I am its life.

I can't remember a time when I didn't have this practice. I even remember dinner table conversations as a kid where we shared what we were grateful for or passing gratitude journals around in high school. It is integrated into my being, and I find so much purpose for my life sharing it with you all.

I also always felt it funny to have or produce a gratitude journal. Like, do we really need it? What's wrong with a pen and paper....

And after more than a decade of sharing prompts, running 30 day gratitude challenge groups and just overall talking about it, here I am working on this new tool for us.

I've been working on prompts for years, I think they help us go a little deeper. They are light posts to help you stop for a moment and reflect along the path. I love that about this journal. I hope it meets you where you are and helps you get to where you want to go.

I've decided to break it down into quarters, or seasons rather. I often talk about these seasons - that is life. The season of growth or grief or parenting or building or rest. They are all seasons.

This journal is meant to be here as a guide. It's a tool in your toolbox. I also believe this practice is the most expansive way to grow your heart and your hope.

Every day reflecting on a moment of good, a ray of light, a glimmer of hope. While also allowing the work, the grief, the heartache, to be there and be present. See that's this practice. It is not whitewashed. It is.

It is both.
It is the inhale & the exhale.
It is always the AND.

I share that gratitude always allows the hurt or grief to be present, it doesn't say "Don't be sad." It says, "It's ok, be sad AND notice the clean sheets on the bed, your partner bringing you tea, the lady who held the door open when you were running late to your meeting."

I hope these three months of practice lead to the next three months and the next three months and the next three months and so on and so on until it's integrated into your being too.

Imagine all of us alive and grateful.

Ahh before we begin on this adventure today, here are a few rules.

There is no right or wrong way to do this book.

You can find something to be grateful for every day. Right now it may feel daunting, but do the work to build the muscle.

Some prompts may feel hard. It's ok. Let it be hard. Take a deep breath and remember you can do hard things.

Just begin. Today.

Some days are more directed than others. Some are just general 'what are you grateful for' prompts. All are important.

I am grateful for you being here with me and on these pages.

Day 1:

Let's begin. First and foremost take a big, deep breath. Today is the first day of something amazing, and I am so proud of you for being here.

That's it, what are 5 things you are grateful for at this moment?
I am grateful for:

1.

2.

3.

4.

5.

Day 2:

Take a deep breath. Come be present with me for this moment.

I am grateful for my big heart and the glasses that spark joy for me. I am grateful for being a good typer, my feet that take me wherever I want to go, and Grubbs' thighs that often feel too big but are just right. I am grateful for hugs and being a good mom.

Please name 7 things you are grateful for about yourself.

1.

2.

3.

4.

5.

6.

7.

Day 3:

Take a deep breath. Fill up your heart and your belly. Now let out a deep exhale, letting it all go for this moment.

What are 4 things about TODAY you are grateful for?

1.

2.

3.

4.

Day 4:

Are you catching on yet? Take a deep breath in.
Be present for this moment.

From right here where you are standing or sitting, can you look around
and find 6 things to be grateful for?

1.

2.

3.

4.

5.

6.

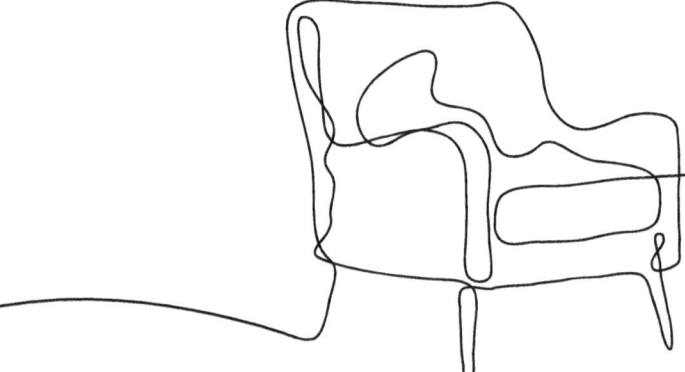

Day 5:

Inhale. Exhale.

What are you grateful for today?

1.

2.

3.

4.

5.

Day 6:

Today I just want you to notice. Be here. Take Notice.

Can you sit with your breath and say thank you.

Day 7:

You did it. You made it through one week. Today, list out as many things as you can that you are grateful for. Be mindful to not repeat anything you've written yet. Empty your heart. Take a big, deep breath.
Can you find 3 more things to add?

1.

2.

3.

4.

5.

6.

7.

8.

9.

10.

11.

12.

13.

14.

15.

Day 8:

Are you in a relationship? What are 3 things about your partner that you are grateful for?

If you are single, what are 3 things about your last relationship that you are grateful for?

1.

2.

3.

Day 9:

What are 7 things you are grateful for about your home?
Look around and take notice of the items you've collected, your favorite
sweater, a warm bed.

1.

2.

3.

4.

5.

6.

7.

Day 10:

Think of your person, the friend you call in the middle of the night or the first person you want to talk to when your day begins. See them?
Feel them sitting next to you?

Let's show some gratitude for them.

What are 8 things about them that you are grateful for?
Take a step further and shoot them a text letting them know you are grateful for them.

1.

2.

3.

4.

5.

6.

7.

8.

Day 11:

What are you grateful for today?

1.

2.

3.

4.

5.

Day 12:

I am super blessed I get to do work I love, and I hope you are, too.
Every Friday, I recap my week with a gratitude list and it's always cup-
filling to look back and see who I got to talk to and work with that week.
Let's take a moment and reflect on your work week.

Can you list 10 things you are grateful for from your work?

1.

2.

3.

4.

5.

6.

7.

8.

9.

10.

Day 13:

Bring it back home here for a second. I want you to name 3 things about yourself you are grateful for—try to not repeat anything from Day 2.

1.

2.

3.

Day 14:

TWO WHOLE WEEKS. Congratulations. I am so proud of you for choosing this practice.

What are 14 things you are grateful for?

1.

2.

3.

4.

5.

6.

7.

8.

9.

10.

11.

12.

13.

14.

GIVE
YOURSELF
GRACE
TODAY

 RACHEL DESROCHERS

Express your creativity and how you're feeling by coloring in the affirmation above.

Day 15:

What are 3 things about your mom you are grateful for?

(If this question feels particularly challenging I just want to remind you what a gift it is having you here. And if nothing else, YOU are something to be grateful for from them.)

1.

2.

3.

Day 16:

Take a big, deep breath, be here. Take Notice.

Can you be grateful for your eyes that see the world?

Day 17:

What are you grateful for today?

1.

2.

3.

4.

5.

6.

7.

Day 18:

What are 3 things in your refrigerator that you are grateful for?

(Does that seem silly? Good. When's the last time you acknowledged the food you have to nourish yourself with?)

1.

2.

3.

Day 19:

Just checking in, are you taking a big deep breath? Ahhh.
Fill up that heart space, fill up that belly.
Nice slow exhale.

What feels heavy right now? Something keeping you up at night?
Not sure what to wear to an event next week?

Just take a moment and put it here.

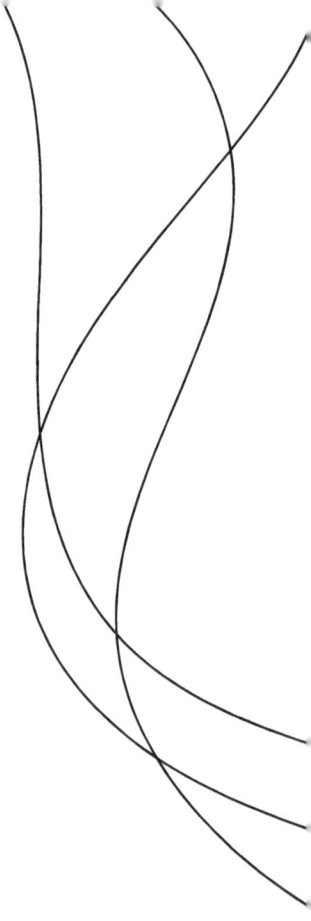

Day 20:

Yesterday you took a moment to put something heavy down.
I hope that you feel a bit better today.

Today take a moment and find 3 things about that heavy thing that you
can be grateful for.

1.

2.

3.

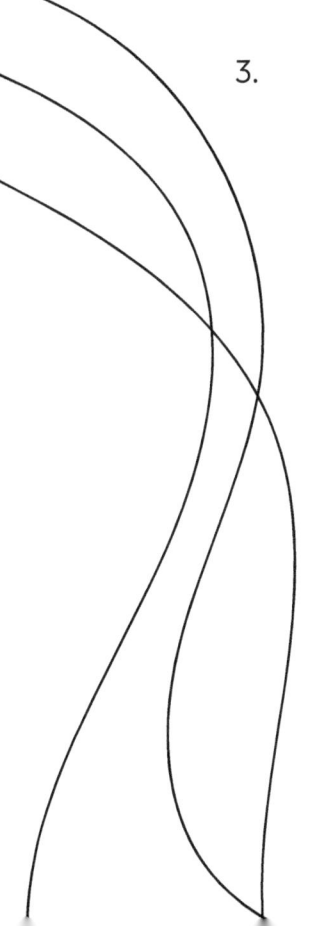

Day 21:

Just acknowledging you here for three weeks. The last 2 days may have been a bit uncomfortable, but that is a reminder you are safe and you are learning to make room for the AND.

What are you grateful for today?

1.

2.

3.

4.

5.

Day 22:

What are 3 things about your dad you are grateful for?

(If this question feels challenging I just want to remind you what a gift it is having you here. And if nothing else, YOU are something to be grateful for from them.)

1.

2.

3.

Day 23:

What are 3 things about outside you are grateful for?

1.

2.

3.

Day 24:

From where you sit...

Take a moment to get present. What are 5 things you are grateful for that you can see from where you sit?

1.

2.

3.

4.

5.

Day 25:

Hope. What is something you are hopeful for right now?
Something you are working on or towards?

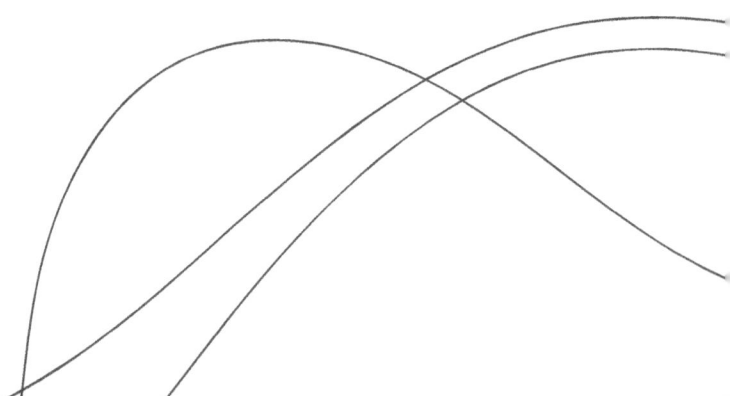

Day 26:

Take a big deep breath, be here. Take notice.
Can you be grateful for your ears that hear the world?

Day 27:

What are you grateful for today? Can you name 15 things that you've not mentioned before?

1.

2.

3.

4.

5.

6.

7.

8.

9.

10.

11.

12.

13.

14.

15.

Day 28:

Do you have siblings? (If you don't, what about a best friend?!)
What are you grateful for about your siblings?
Can you name them each and 3 things about each of them?

Name:

1.

2.

3.

Name:

1.

2.

3.

Name:

1.

2.

3.

Name:

1.

2.

3.

Day 29:

Extended family. Think about your grandparents or aunt or uncle. Who is it? Who is the first person that pops up when you think about them?

Name:

Why were they the first person?

What are 3 things about them you are grateful for?

1.

2.

3.

Day 30:

And just like that you've completed a month of gratitude.
How do you feel?

Ready for a challenge? Let's flex that muscle you've been working on! Below please list 30 things you are grateful for.

1.

2.

3.

4.

5.

6.

7.

8.

9.

10.

11.

12.

13.

14.

15.

16.

17.

18.

19.

20.

21.

22.

23.

24.

25.

26.

27.

28.

29.

30.

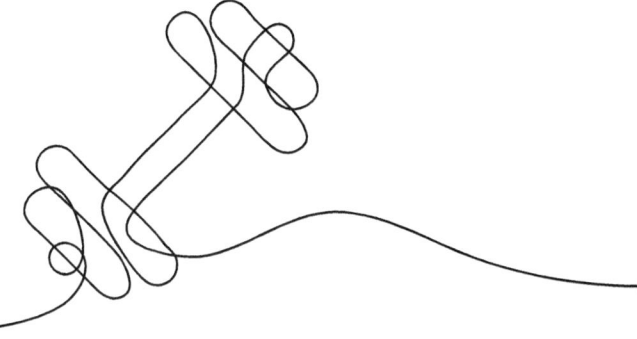

LET THE JOURNEY BUILD YOU

 RACHEL DESROCHERS

Express your creativity and how you're feeling by coloring in the affirmation above.

Day 31:

Today please text 2 people and let them know you are grateful for them.

Who did you text?

1.

2.

Day 32:

What are you grateful for today?

1.

2.

3.

4.

5.

Day 33:

Inhale. Connect in with your heart.
Can you sit here for 60 seconds just breathing? In. Out. Slowly.

Just take a moment in stillness. Just be grateful for you & the breath.

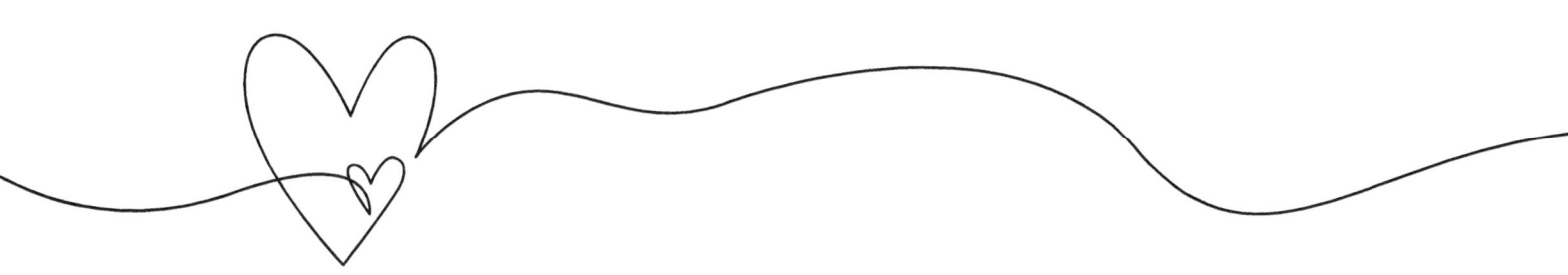

Day 34:

Treasures. Don't we all have things we've collected that fill our home with moments and memories?

Take a look around. Acknowledge where you have come and where you are going.

Name 5 treasures you are grateful for.

1.

2.

3.

4.

5.

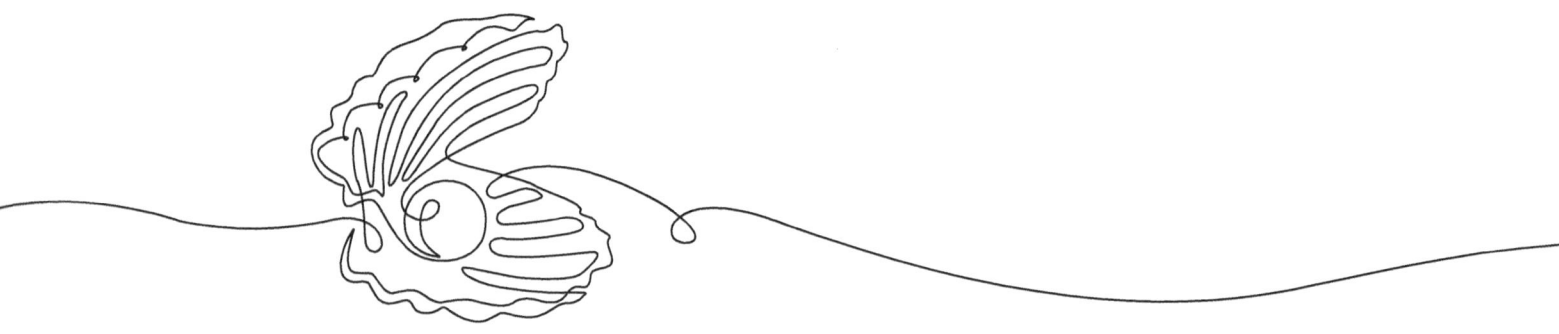

Day 35:

Community. Are you on the PTA or do you belong to a women's group?
Do you have a book club or yoga studio you are part of?
List the people you are in community with, giving thanks for them and
what they bring to your life! Next to each name, write two or three
things about them that you are grateful for.

Name/Group:

1.

2.

3.

Name/Group:

1.

2.

3.

Name/Group:

1.

2.

3.

Day 36:

What are you grateful for?

1.

2.

3.

4.

5.

Day 37:

I imagine we all have things about ourselves that we don't love. I complain about my thighs or not knowing how to do something or my belly which maybe I feel jiggles too much! Can you take a moment here and list those things. I think it's powerful to acknowledge it. To say it out loud.

1.

2.

3.

4.

5.

Day 38:

Take a look at yesterday's prompt. Sit with it for a moment here.
The thighs or crooked teeth or the grief.

I want you to find at least 1 thing to be grateful for about each of the
things you listed. For example, yesterday I mentioned my belly & I am so
grateful it held 3 incredible children that I am now a mom to. A gift.

1.

2.

3.

4.

5.

Day 39:

Take a big deep breath, be here. Take notice.

Can you be grateful for your tongue that tastes the flavors of the world?

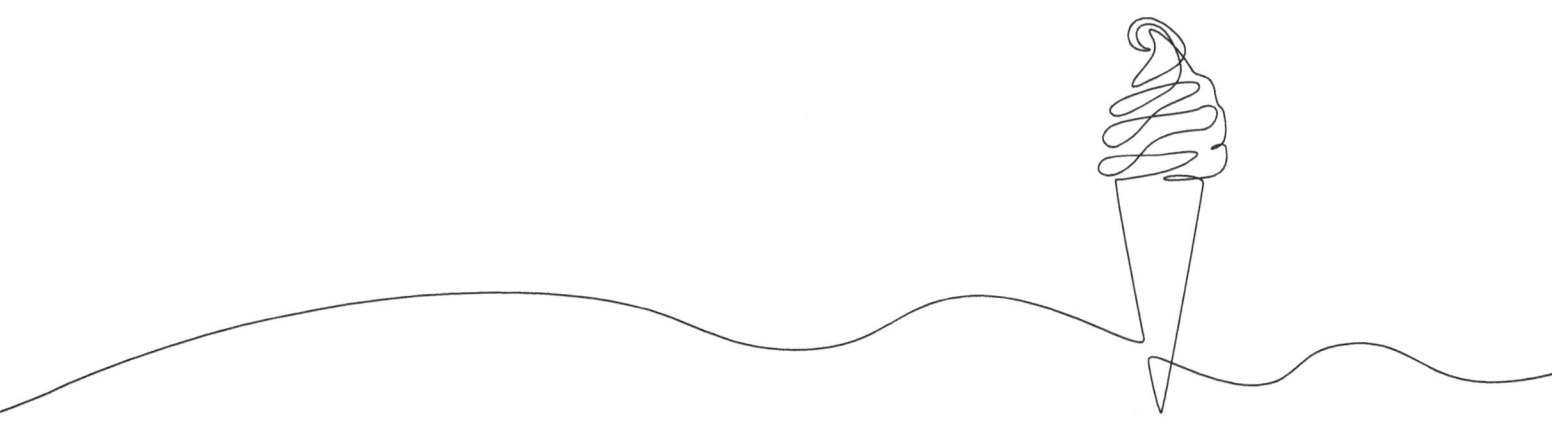

Day 40:

Please send a text to someone today or send a meal or an email or—gasp—make a phone call and let someone know you are grateful for them. There is something about the additional action here - the gratitude in action that keeps making those ripples grow, an impact to be made.

Who did you message or call?

1.

Day 41:

Write about a family tradition, new or old, that you are grateful to be doing and carrying on!

Day 42:

A follow up from last week's entry about the good & the bad of you, your body etc. I just want to revisit that for a moment.

The Power of Positivity. Take more time to think about YOU and now reframe anything that's less than glowing. Please list all the body positive words and kind things you can think of about yourself. And keep adding to this list. Don't stop. Friends, we can never have too many reminders about how good and how enough we are!

1.

2.

3.

4.

5.

6.

7.

8.

9.

10.

Day 43:

Inhale - 4 seconds in
Exhale - 8 seconds out

Can you sit here in this breath for 1 minute? 3 Minutes? 5 minutes?

Can you hold space for yourself today to just connect with your heart?
Let's give our hearts some gratitude today!

Feel free to journal anything that is coming up for you:

Day 44:

Today's gratitude challenge - What is one form of self care you can do for yourself today?

Do it, then write out what you did to show yourself a little gratitude today!

Day 45:

What are 12 things you are grateful for today?

Can you list 12 new things that you've not shared yet in our past 44 days together?

1.

2.

3.

4.

5.

6.

7.

8.

9.

10.

11.

12.

Day 46:

Who is someone who hurt you?
Do you still carry that hurt around with you?
Let's acknowledge this person here.

Name:

What did they do to hurt you?

Just let it be. You don't have to keep carrying it.

Day 47:

Can you list 2 things about the person from yesterday that you are grateful for? What are 2 things? That you are no longer with the person, even that counts.

A little light can go a long way.

1.

2.

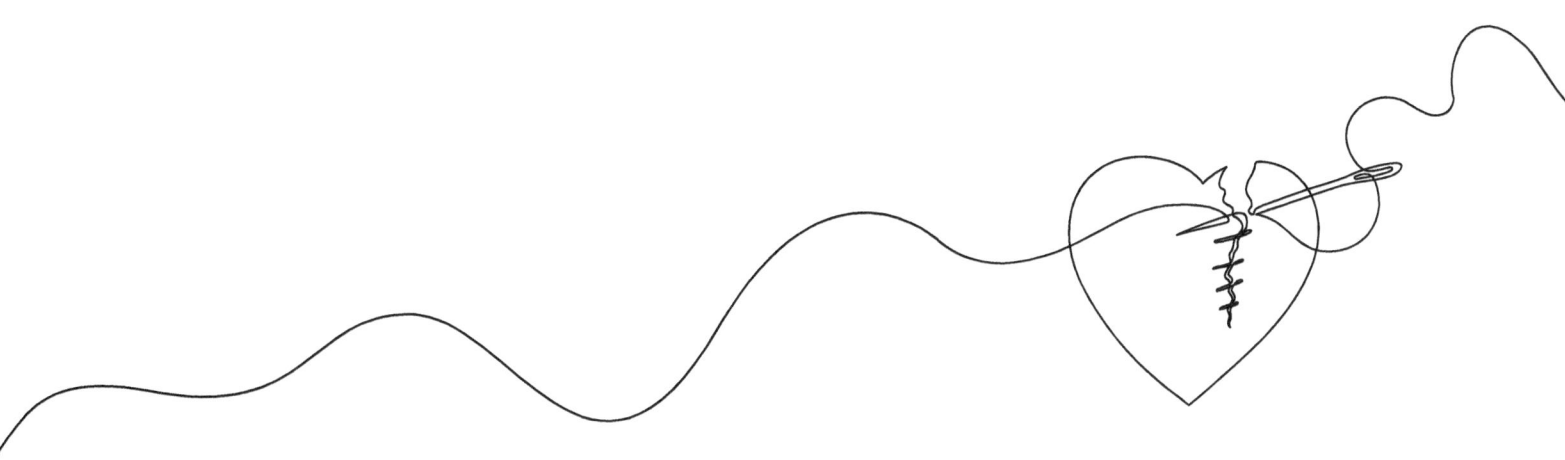

Day 48:

From your bed.

I love my bed. It's my sanctuary in this season. One of my best friends, Tara, came over after my divorce and helped me create my sanctuary. A room I could feel safe & restored. I am grateful for her.

Now, what about you? From your bed, can you see 5 things you are grateful for just in your bedroom?

1.

2.

3.

4.

5.

Day 49:

Take a big deep breath, be here. Take notice.

Can you be grateful for your hands that feel the world?

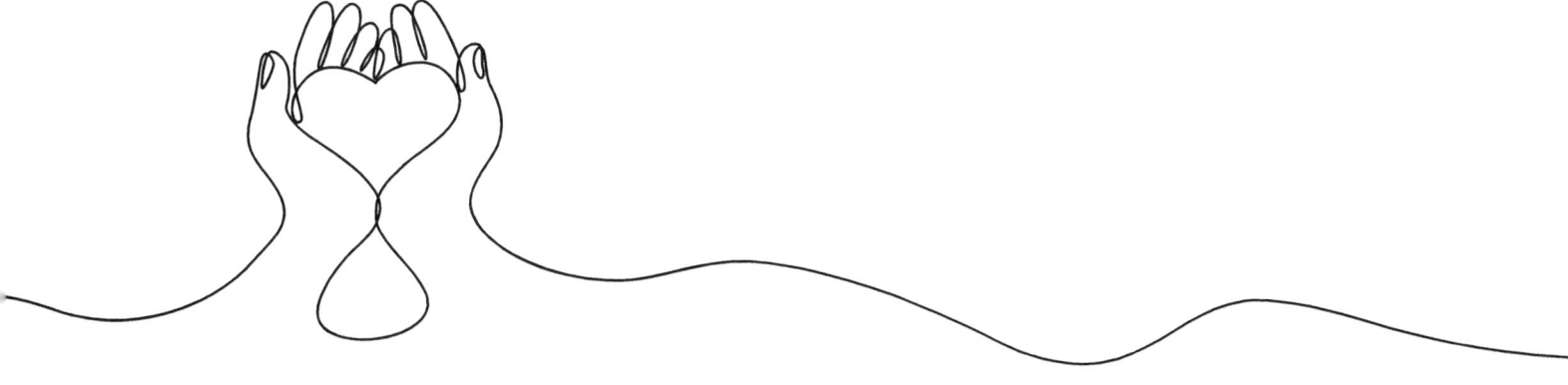

Day 50:

What is 1 thing you are grateful for at this very moment?

1.

Day 51:

What are 7 things you are grateful for?

1.

2.

3.

4.

5.

6.

7.

Day 52:

What are you grateful for in your neighborhood?

A favorite tree or coffee shop, a hidden hiking trail or a neighbor.

Can you list 3 things in your neighborhood you are grateful for?

1.

2.

3.

Day 53:

Take a big deep breath and just relax. Fill up your heart, fill up your belly. Slow exhale. And again.

Today I challenge you to say THANK YOU. Put this practice in action.

Thanks for the food you are eating. Thanks for the clean water you are drinking. Thanks to your family for helping. Thanks to your coworker for solving a problem with you.

How many times did you give thanks today?

Day 54:

Take note right from where you are sitting or standing.

What are 3 things you see that you are grateful for?

1.

2.

3.

Day 55:

Take a deep breath in. How do you feel 55 days into this practice?
Has your hope expanded? Has your heart expanded?

Keep going! Keep going!

What is something you've learned in your 55 days of practicing gratitude?

Day 56:

What is your favorite activity to do? What do you love about it?

What are 3 things about the activity that you are grateful for?

1.

2.

3.

Day 57:

What are you grateful for about your week?

List as many things you can think of.

1.

2.

3.

4.

5.

6.

7.

8.

9.

10.

11.

12.

13.

14.

15.

Day 58:

What are 3 things you are grateful for about yourself?

1.

2.

3.

Day 59:

Self care. What is one self care you can do for yourself today?
How do you show yourself some gratitude?

Day 60:

Incredible. Two months of practicing. Of allowing. Of showing up for yourself. Here is today's challenge or an opportunity. This may take you a couple of hours or the entire day to work through, but I think you are up for the challenge.

Can you name 60 things you are grateful for?

1.

2.

3.

4.

5.

6.

7.

8.

9.

10.

11.

12.

13.

14.

15.

16.

17.

18.

19.

20.

21.

22.

23.

24.

25.

26.

27.

28.

29.

30.

31.

32.

33.

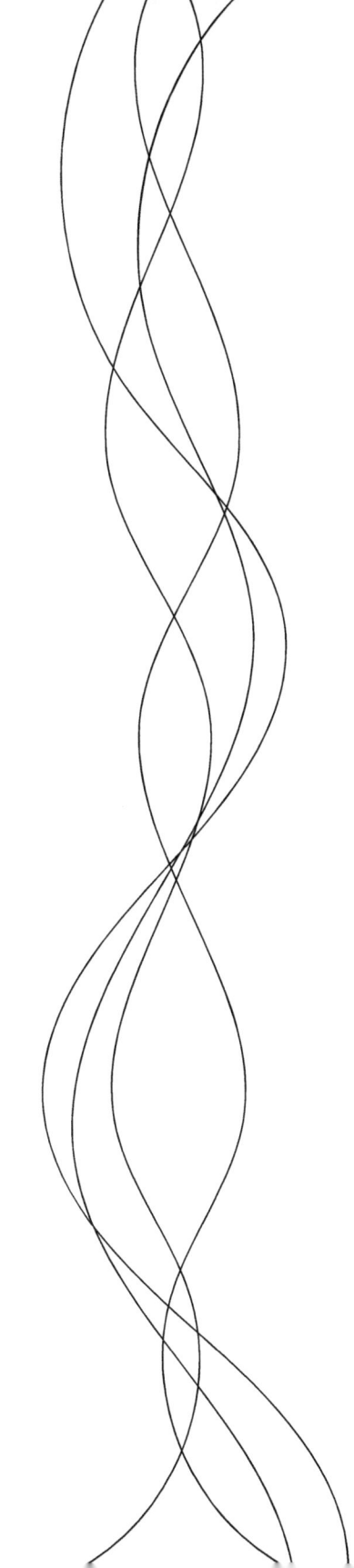

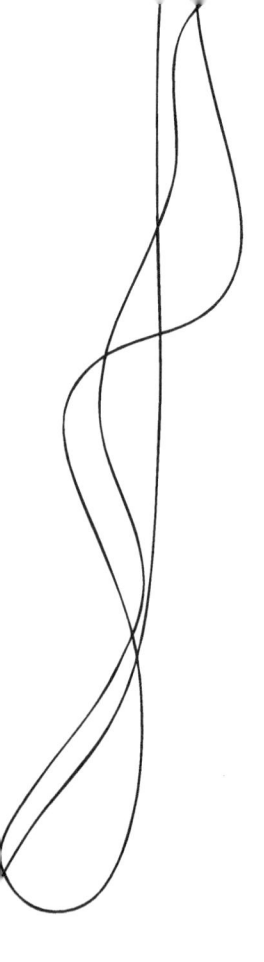

34.

35.

36.

37.

38.

39.

40.

41.

42.

43.

44.

45.

46.

47.

48.

49.

50.

51.

52.

53.

54.

55.

56.

57.

58.

59.

60.

Wow, your gratitude muscle is getting so strong! Way to go.

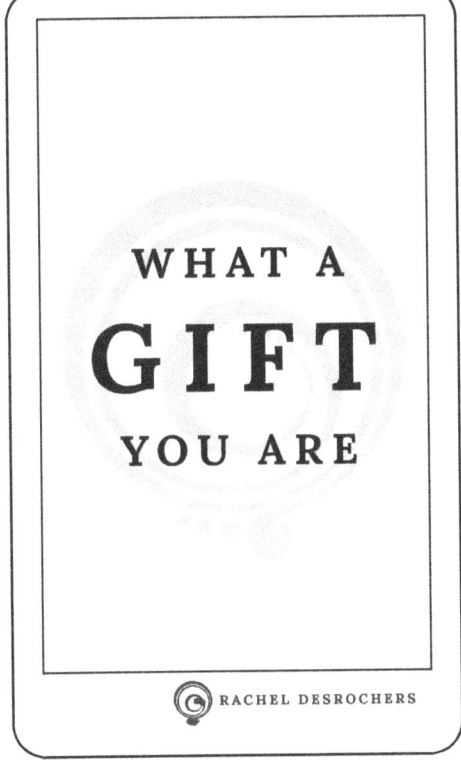

Express your creativity and how you're feeling by coloring in this affirmation.

Day 61:

Have a few spots left to fill from yesterday?

Then go fill in a few more lines. Go outside, feel the sunshine on your face and acknowledge your work in this practice.

Day 62:

What is this season like for you? Is work really busy? Do the kids have a ton going on? Are you grieving a loss? Is this a season of rest?

How are you feeding yourself in this season?

Day 63:

Write something you are grateful for from each letter?

G

R

A

T

E

F

U

L

Day 64:

What are 5 things you are grateful for about how you grew up?

A lesson learned, a memory, or moment.

1.

2.

3.

4.

5.

Day 65:

You allowed yourself to talk about your hope.

What are 3 things about what you are working on or towards that you are grateful for?

1.

2.

3.

Day 66:

What are you grateful for today?

1.

2.

3.

4.

5.

6.

7.

8.

9.

10.

Day 67:

Let's take a walk. In your backyard, around the block, or on your favorite trail.

I want you to be present. I want you to notice what it feels like outside. What do you smell? Is the wind blowing? Can you be present during your walk, no matter how long.

What are 3 things you noticed during your walk?

1.

2.

3.

Day 68:

Take a big deep breath, be here. Take notice.

Can you be grateful for your nose that smells the world?

Day 69:

What are you grateful for today?

1.

2.

3.

Day 70:

Seventy days of changing your life. Congratulations!

I want you to capture everything that made you smile today. Take notice. Be present. The wave from the mailman, a text from a friend, a cup of coffee from a coworker.

What made you smile today?

Day 71:

What are 3 things about where you are in this very moment that you are grateful for? Perhaps this moment of life or this very moment from where you stand.

1.

2.

3.

Day 72:

On the next page, write your name (like this).

R

A

C

H

E

L

Write one thing you are grateful for, whether about yourself or about life in general.

Mine in this moment would say:

R - Rosie, my daughter and our relationship

A - Apples

C - Camden, this season of having him home

H - Hugs, Goodness I love hugs

E - Ellis, what a gift he is

L - Love, I love love. I love it.

Day 72:

Write your name.

Day 73:

What's your favorite piece of clothing that you own? What do you love about it? How does it make you feel?

I'd say 1 of my top 10 favorites is this beautiful hand knitted scarf from my friend Alicia, she thought of me, picked out favorite colors. It has gold threads woven in and makes me feel warm & loved.

What about you?

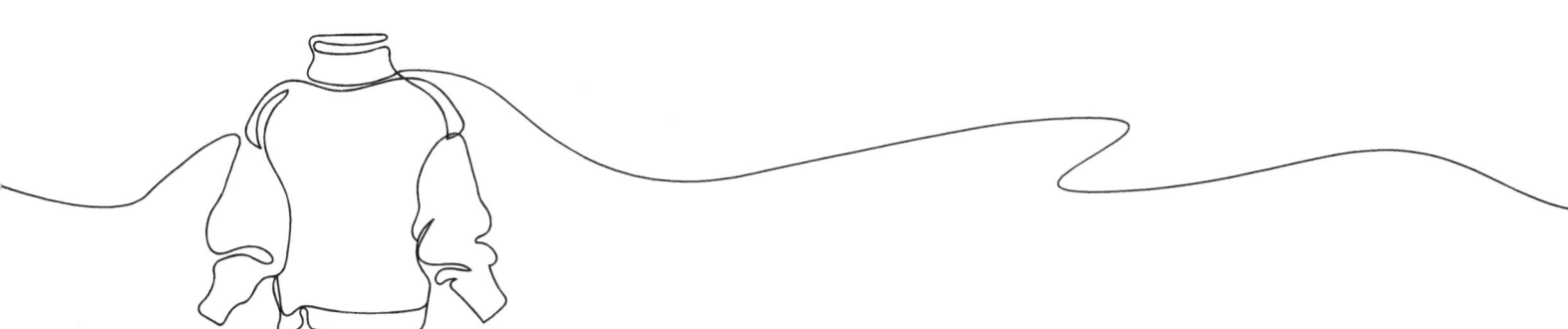

Day 74:

What are 7 things you are grateful for today?

1.

2.

3.

4.

5.

6.

7.

Day 75:

Who is the first person that comes to mind?

Shoot them a text & let them know you are grateful for them!

Day 76:

How did it make you feel when you sent that text yesterday?

How do you think the recipient felt?

Day 77:

What are you grateful for today?

1.

2.

3.

Day 78:

Take a few moments and think about yesterday. Spend a few minutes and walk slowly, start to finish your day, waking up, getting coffee made, getting up, getting ready, your day, coming back home, etc., etc...

What moments do you recall that you wouldn't have noticed without taking this pause?

1.

2.

3.

Day 79:

If you do this activity in the morning... What are you hopeful for today?

If you do this activity in the evening... What are you hopeful for tomorrow?

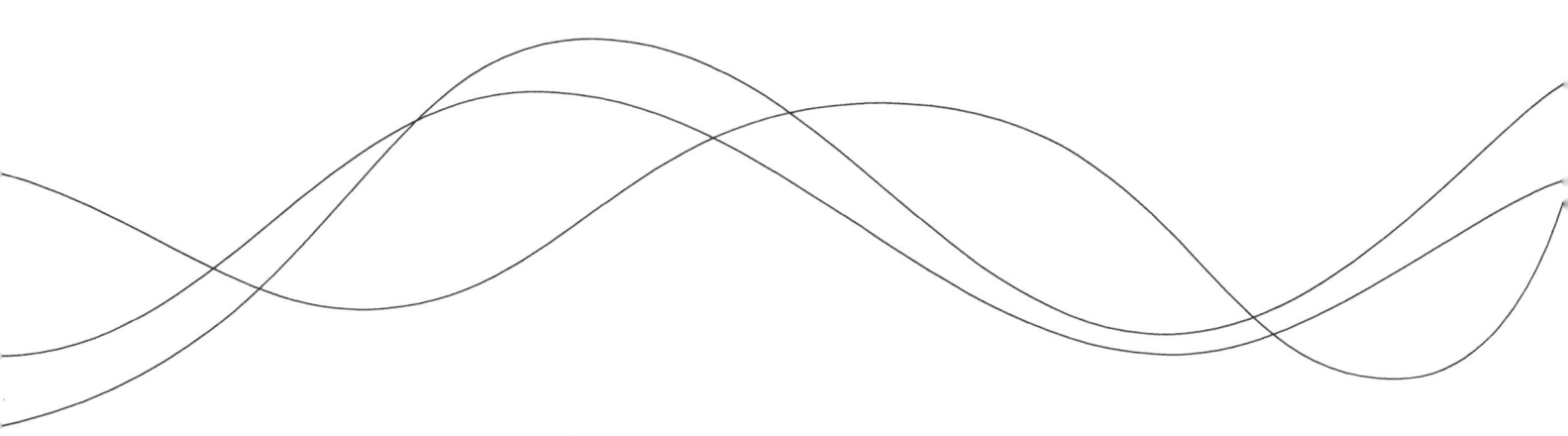

Day 80:

How did yesterday work out for you? On the thing you were hopeful for...

Your partner emptied the dishwasher without being asked
A raise at work
Dinner with a friend
Good news from the doctor

Did it turn out the way you wanted it to? Expected it to?

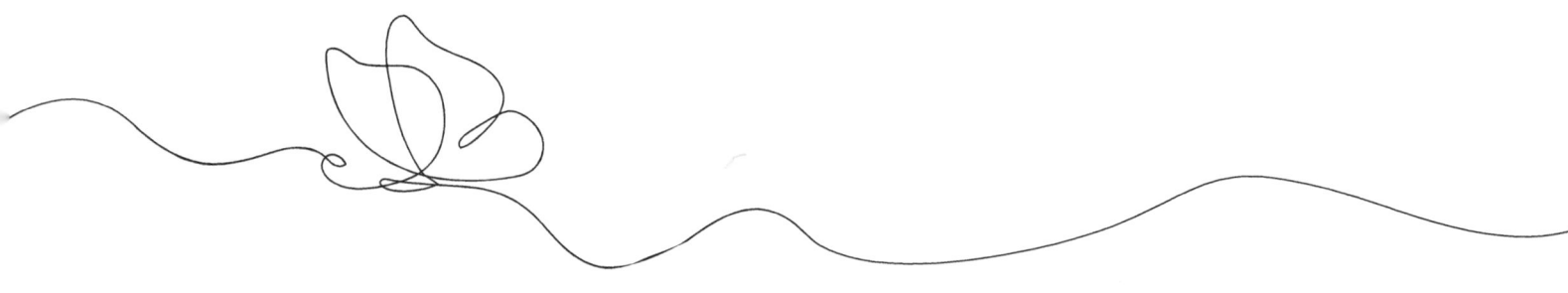

Day 81:

No matter how yesterday went, can you find 3 things to be grateful for? The experience, the fact that you were happy the friend canceled so you could have a quiet night, etc.

1.

2.

3.

Day 82:

What are you grateful for today?

1.

2.

3.

4.

5.

Day 83:

Pause, take notice.
From this moment, can you take a big deep breath, fill up your heart & belly.
Hold for 3 seconds, and slowly exhale.

Be here. Again with a deep breath. Can you do that 5 times?
Just keep filling your heart & belly, hold 3 seconds, then exhale
..... s l o w l y.

Day 84:

What's one memory of gratitude from when you started this practice 83 days ago?

Day 85:

A challenge.

Can you write or email (but come on, how fun are hand written cards) someone who is on your heart or mind. Let them know you are thinking of them, something about them you miss, letting them know what's new with you. Just take a moment and share the light you've been busy cultivating with another.

Who did you write to?

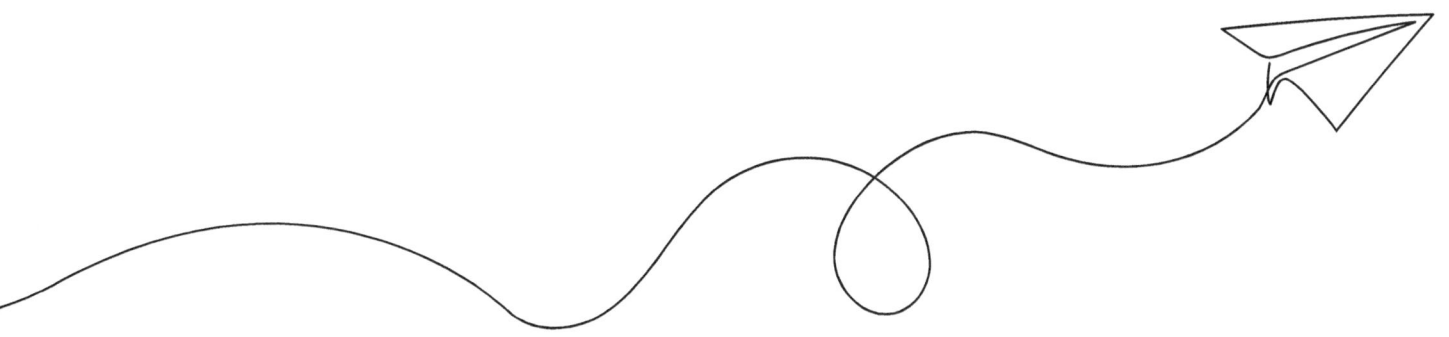

Day 86:

What's the nicest thing someone has ever done for you?

What's the nicest thing you have ever done for someone?

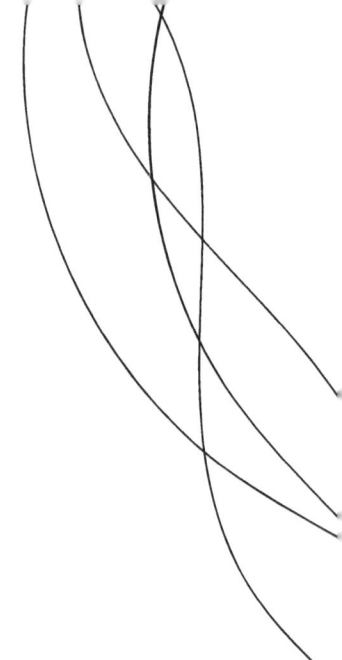

Day 87:

What is one thing from the last week that you are grateful for?

1.

Day 88:

Where is your favorite place you have traveled to? Why?

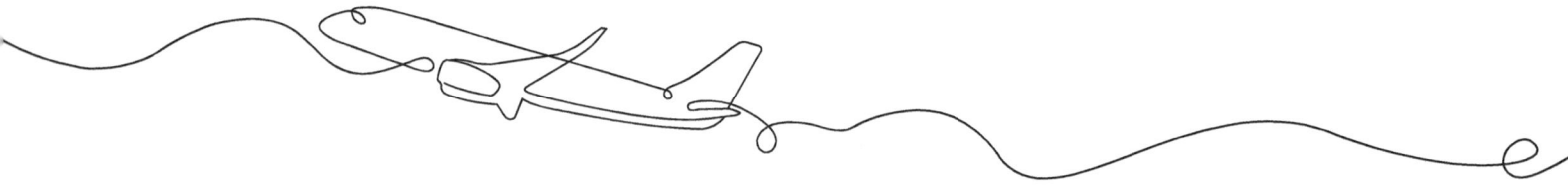

Day 89:

What are 5 things about your favorite place from yesterday that you are grateful for?

1.

2.

3.

4.

5.

Day 90:

And just like that you've been practicing for 90 days.

First & foremost - a round of applause for you & this practice.

I am so grateful you did it!

Now... can you name 30, 60, 90 things to be grateful for. Take your time, perhaps write until you can't write any longer, and then come back the next day & the next day continuing your list & your practice until you've reached 90 things!

1.

2.

3.

4.

5.

6.

7.

8.

9.

10.

11.

12.

13.

14.

15.

16.

17.

18.

19.

20.

21.

22.

23.

24.

25.

26.

27.

28.

29.

30.

31.

32.

33.

34.

35.

36.

37.

38.

39.

40.

41.

42.

43.

44.

45.

46.

47.

48.

49.

50.

51.

52.

53.

54.

55.

56.

57.

58.

59.

60.

61.

62.

63.

64.

65.

66.

67.

68.

69.

70.

71.

72.

73.

74.

75.

76.

77.

78.

79.

80.

81.

82.

83.

84.

85.

86.

87.

88.

89.

90.

WHAT BRINGS
YOU JOY?

DO
MORE
OF THAT

 RACHEL DESROCHERS

Express your creativity and how you're feeling
by coloring in the affirmation above.

YOU ARE
NOT
ALONE

RACHEL DESROCHERS

Express your creativity and how you're feeling by
coloring in the affirmation above.

And just like that, you've completed 90 days of gratitude!

I am so proud of you. The time, effort & practice, what a way to love yourself.

I hope this journal met you where you were & perhaps helped you take a step or two towards where you want to go. I hope this journal expanded your heart, reminding you of possibility. I hope this journal helped you shed a layer or two, the great evolving. I hope this journal brought comfort & joy, held pain & nurtured you through it.

Thank you, it's the honor of a lifetime to share this journal with you.

In Gratitude,

Rachel

Stay tuned for another version in the future, but I won't tell if you choose to do this one over a time or two! ♡

Congratulations on strengthening your gratitude muscle!

FIND GRATITUDE TODAY

 RACHEL DESROCHERS

Express your creativity and how you're feeling
by coloring in the affirmation above.

About VITALITY

VITALITY is a circle of friends welcoming all, awakening each other, and reminding each other that we are Whole. Our affordable self-care programs invite everyone to move, to breathe, to rest, to contemplate, to grow...wherever each person begins their self-care journey, wherever and however they want to become.

Donation-based drop-in classes... in person & via Zoom

Affordable trainings

Individual sessions

Volunteer opportunities

vitalitycincinnati.org

Publishing books from VITALITY's circle of friends
inspiring love, creativity, + possibility
vitalitybuzz.org